TEXAS Rangers

BY ALEX MONNIG

Published by The Child's World®
1980 Lookout Drive • Mankato, MN 56003-1705
800-599-READ • www.childsworld.com

Acknowledgments
The Child's World®: Mary Berendes, Publishing Director
Red Line Editorial: Editorial direction
The Design Lab: Design
Amnet: Production
Design Elements: Photodisc

Photographs ©: Kevin Hill Illustration/Shutterstock Images,
cover, 1, 2; Zuma Press/Icon SMI, 5, 10, 25 (bottom); Daniel
Gluskoter/Icon SMI, 6; AP Images, 9, 22 (inset); Shutterstock
Images, 13; Design Lab, 14; Charlie Riedel/AP Images, 17; Ben
Margot/AP Images, 18; Kyodo/AP Images, 21; LM Otero/AP
Images, 22; Ray Carlin/Icon SMI, 25 (top), 25 (center); Steven
King/Icon SMI, 26; Andrew Dieb/Icon SMI, 27

ISBN 9781623239800
LCCN 2013947266

Printed in the United States of America
Mankato, MN
December, 2013
PA02188

ABOUT THE AUTHOR

Alex Monnig is a journalist who has covered sporting events around the world and written more than a dozen sports books for young readers. Even though he is sometimes far from home, he always follows his favorite team, the St. Louis Cardinals.

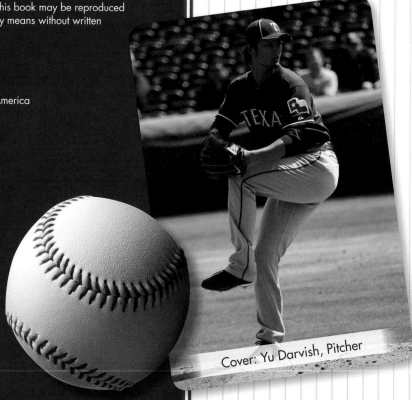

Cover: Yu Darvish, Pitcher

CONTENTS

Go, Rangers!

The Texas Rangers are one of baseball's most exciting teams. They have not been around as long as some other teams, but that has not stopped them from becoming a popular team in the southern part of the United States. Texas has never won a **World Series**, but they continue to get closer. Let's meet the Rangers!

Craig Gentry (left) congratulates Mitch Moreland on his two-run home run in a game against the Oakland Athletics.

Who Are the Rangers?

The Texas Rangers are a team in baseball's American League (AL). The AL joins with the National League (NL) to form Major League Baseball. The Rangers play in the West Division of the AL. The division winners and two wild-card teams get to play in the league playoffs. The playoff winners from the two leagues face off in the World Series. The Rangers have played in two World Series.

Third baseman Adrian Beltre follows through on a swing in a game against the Athletics.

Where They Came From

The Texas Rangers weren't always the Texas Rangers. At first they weren't even from Texas! In 1961 the Washington Senators were created. But people in the nation's capital quickly lost interest in the losing team. Major League Baseball wanted a team in north Texas, so the Senators moved before the 1972 season and became the Texas Rangers!

Ted Williams was manager of the new Texas Rangers team in 1972.

Who They Play

The Texas Rangers play 162 games each season. That includes about 19 games against each of the other teams in their division. The Rangers have won six AL West championships. The other AL West teams are the Oakland Athletics, the Los Angeles Angels of Anaheim, the Seattle Mariners, and the Houston Astros. The Rangers and the Angels are two of baseball's biggest **rivals**. Their games always get fans charged up! They both are willing to spend money to bring in the best players. The Rangers also play some teams from the NL. Their NL opponents change every year.

Leonys Martin steals second base in a game against the Los Angeles Angels.

Where They Play

Rangers Ballpark in Arlington, Texas, is home to the Texas Rangers. It opened on April 1, 1994, when Texas played the New York Mets in an exhibition game. The first regular-season game was played ten days later against the Milwaukee Brewers. The stadium holds more than 49,000 fans and is part of a larger complex that features offices and games for kids.

Rangers fans fill the seats of Rangers Ballpark to cheer for their team.

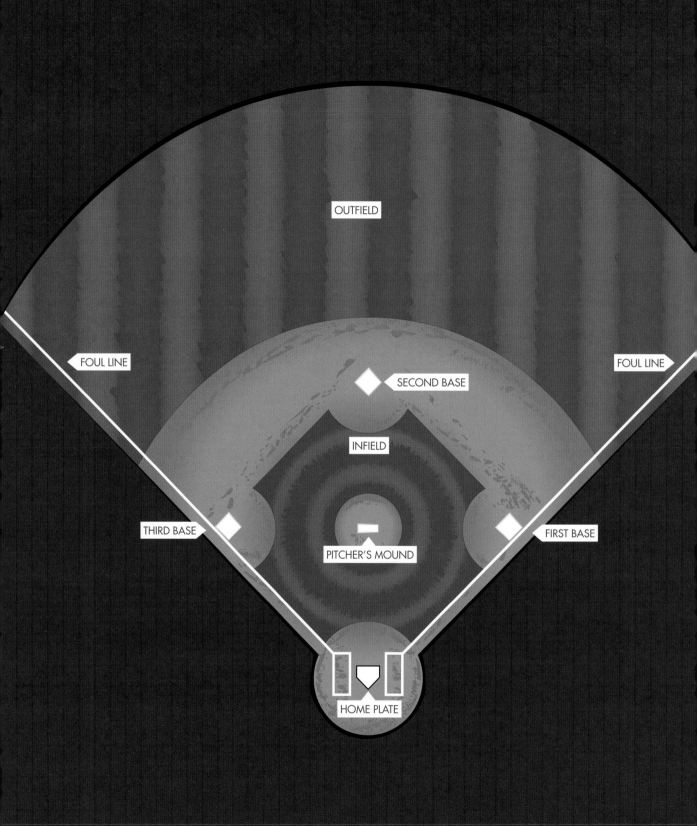

The Baseball Diamond

Baseball games are played on a field called a diamond. Four bases form this diamond shape. The bases are 90 feet (27 m) apart. The area around and between the bases is called the infield. At the center of the infield is the pitcher's mound. The grass area beyond the bases is called the outfield. White lines start at **home plate** and go toward the outfield. These are the foul lines. Baseballs hit outside these lines are out of play unless they are caught by a fielder. The outfield walls are about 300–450 feet (91–137 m) from home plate.

Big Days

The Rangers have had some great seasons in their short history. Here are three of the greatest:

1996: *The Rangers won 90 games and captured the AL West for the first time. They made their first playoff appearance, but lost in the first round to the New York Yankees.*

2010: *In its 50th season, Texas made its first World Series appearance. They lost the World Series to the San Francisco Giants.*

2011: *The Rangers won a team-record 96 games and made their second World Series appearance in a row. This time, the St. Louis Cardinals defeated them.*

Rangers players celebrate on the field after winning the AL Championship Series in 2011.

Tough Days

Baseball seasons can't always go well. Here are some of the toughest seasons in Rangers history:

1963: *As the Washington Senators, the team lost 106 games, which is still a single-season franchise record.*

2011: *Even though it was a good year, it was also maybe the most painful. The Rangers had the St. Louis Cardinals down to their last strike twice in Game 6 of the World Series, but they just couldn't close the deal. The Cardinals won in seven games.*

2012: *This was another great season that fell apart late. Texas lost a big AL West lead at the end of the year to the Oakland Athletics before losing to the Baltimore Orioles in the AL Wild Card Game.*

Texas Rangers' manager Ron Washington can't watch as his team loses to the Oakland Athletics in 2012.

Meet the Fans

Loyal Rangers fans have been flocking to the stadium with the team's improvement in the standings. The team ranks near the top of the AL in attendance nearly every year. A horse **mascot** named Rangers Captain was created in 2003. He is dressed in classic Western cowboy gear to honor the history of the state of Texas.

Rangers fans enjoy cheering for their team and favorite players.

Nolan Ryan, Pitcher

Heroes Then . . .

Frank Howard, nicknamed "The Washington Monument," was one of the only Senators stars. He made four **All-Star Game** appearances with Washington and led the league in runs batted in and walks in 1970. Fireballer Nolan Ryan is one of the most famous pitchers ever. He played for the Rangers from 1989 to 1993 and holds the career record for strikeouts with 5,714. Juan Gonzalez is maybe the best power hitter in team history. He won the **Most Valuable Player (MVP)** award in 1996 and 1998. Ivan Rodriguez, Alex Rodriguez, and Josh Hamilton also won an MVP award each with Texas before departing for other teams.

Juan Gonzalez was a strong hitter for the Rangers.

Heroes Now . . .

Today's Texas Rangers are loaded with stars. Second baseman Ian Kinsler is one of the best infielders in baseball. He has been an All-Star three times in his first seven seasons. Third baseman Adrian Beltre is a star at the plate and in the field, hitting 33 home runs and winning a **Gold Glove** award in each of his first two seasons with Texas. Pitcher Yu Darvish is from Japan. He was an All-Star in his first two seasons. Manager Ron Washington leads them. He took the Rangers to the World Series in his fourth and fifth years with Texas. Nolan Ryan is now the team's owner.

The present-day Rangers are loaded with star players.

Adrian Beltre, Third Base

Ian Kinsler, Second Base

Yu Darvish, Pitcher

BATTING HELMET

BATTING GLOVES

TEAM JERSEY

BAT

TEAM PANTS

BASEBALL CLEATS

Gearing Up

Baseball players all wear a team jersey and pants. They have to wear a team hat in the field and a helmet when batting. Take a look at Ian Kinsler and Geovany Soto to see some other parts of a baseball player's uniform.

CATCHER'S MASK

CATCHER'S CHEST PROTECTOR

CATCHER'S MITT

CATCHER'S SHIN GUARD

Geovany Soto, Catcher

On the left: Ian Kinsler, Second Base

Sports Stats

Here are some all-time career records for the Texas Rangers. All the stats are through the 2013 season.

THE BASEBALL

A Major League baseball weighs about 5 ounces (142 g). It is 9 inches (23 cm) around. A leather cover surrounds hundreds of feet of string. That string is wound around a small center of rubber and cork.

HOME RUNS

Juan Gonzalez, 372
Rafael Palmeiro, 321

RUNS BATTED IN

Juan Gonzalez, 1,180
Rafael Palmeiro, 1,039

BATTING AVERAGE

Al Oliver, .319
Adrian Beltre, .312

STOLEN BASES

Ian Kinsler, 172
Elvis Andrus, 165

WINS BY A PITCHER

Charlie Hough, 139
Kenny Rogers, 133

WINS BY A MANAGER

Ron Washington, 611

EARNED RUN AVERAGE

Darold Knowles, 2.46
Bert Blyleven, 2.74

Glossary

All-Star Game a yearly game between the best players in each league. Frank Howard made four All-Star Game appearances.

Gold Glove an award given to the top fielder at each position in each league. Third baseman Adrian Beltre has won two Gold Glove awards.

home plate a five-sided rubber pad where batters stand to swing. Runners touch home plate to score runs.

mascot a person in costume or an animal that helps fans cheer for their team. A horse named Rangers Captain is the Rangers' mascot.

Most Valuable Player (MVP) a yearly award given to the top player in each league. Juan Gonzalez won the MVP award twice.

rivals teams that play each other often and have an ongoing competition. The Rangers and the Angels are rivals.

World Series the Major League Baseball championship. The World Series is played each year between the winners of the American and National Leagues.

Find Out More

BOOKS

Buckley, James Jr. *Eyewitness Baseball.*
New York: DK Publishing, 2010.

Burson, Rusty. *100 Things Rangers Fans Should Know & Do Before They Die.* Chicago, IL: Triumph Books LLC, 2012.

Teitelbaum, Michael. *Baseball*. Ann Arbor,
MI: Cherry Lake Publishing, 2009.

WEB SITES

Visit our Web page for links about the Texas Rangers and other pro baseball teams. *www.childsworld.com/links*

Note to Parents, Teachers, and Librarians: We routinely verify our Web links to make sure they are safe and active sites. So encourage your readers to check them out!

Index